4/24

Francisco Coronado

Discover The Life Of An Explorer

Trish Kline

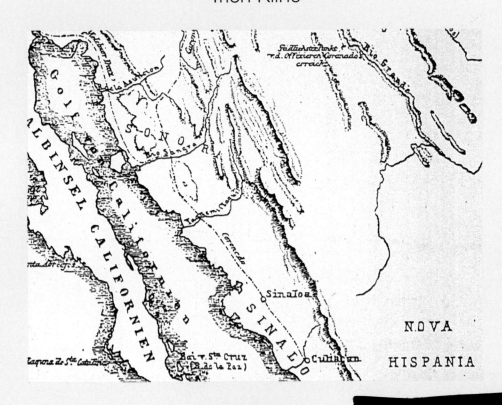

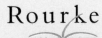

Rourke

Publishing LLC

Vero Beach, Florida 32964

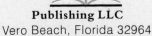

www.rourkepublishing.com

PHOTO CREDITS: IRC-www.historypictures.com: page 8; © Hulton/Archive by
Getty Images: title page, pages 7, 21; © James P. Rowan: pages, 10, 12, 13;
Library of Congress: page 4; © Corbis: cover, pages 15, 18; © Artville: page 17.

Title page: An early map of Spain

Editor: Frank Sloan

Cover design by Nicola Stratford

Library of Congress Cataloging-in-Publication Data

Kline, Trish
    Francisco Coronado / Trish Kline.
        p. cm. — (Discover the life of an explorer)
    Summary: Introduces the life of the sixteenth century Spanish explorer who
    searched for cities of gold in parts of the American Southwest, but discovered
    only Indian villages.
    Includes bibliographical references (p.) and index.
    ISBN 1-58952-294-X
    1. Coronado, Francisco Vâsquez de, 1510-1554—Juvenile literature. 2.
    Explorers—America—Biography—Juvenile literature. 3. Explorers—Spain—
    Biography—Juvenile literature. 4. America—Discovery and exploration—
    Spanish—Juvenile literature. 5. Southwest, New—Discovery and exploration—
    Spanish—Juvenile literature. [1. Coronado, Francisco Vâsquez de, 1510-1554.
    2. Explorers. 3. Southwest, New—Discovery and exploration. 4. America—
    Discovery and exploration—Spanish.] I. Title.

E125.V3 K56 2002
979'.01'092—dc21
[B]   2002017047

Printed in the USA

CG/CG

TABLE OF CONTENTS

VOYAGE TO NEW SPAIN

Francisco Coronado (frahn SEE sko COR uh NAHD oh) was born in Spain in 1510. His family was very rich. At age 25, Coronado traveled to the New World. He worked for the governor of New Spain. New Spain was the present-day country of Mexico.

Soon, Coronado was made the governor of a **territory**. The rulers of New Spain thought that Coronado would become a man of power.

Coronado made the dangerous voyage to the New World in 1535.

A TALE OF GREAT RICHES

In 1540, a slave returned from an **expedition**. The leaders of the expedition had been killed. The slave told stories about cities of gold. The slave said that the ruler of this land took naps under a tree covered with tiny, gold bells. He said the gold bells made music.

King Charles of Spain hoped the explorers would find gold in the New World.

SEVEN CITIES OF GOLD

The governor of New Spain wanted these riches. He sent Coronado to find the Seven Cities of Gold. The governor gave Coronado an army of 1,000 men and 500 horses and mules.

Coronado led an expedition to find the Seven Cities of Gold.

SEARCHING FOR THE CITIES

Coronado traveled north into the land we now know as Texas. Then, he traveled west. Coronado sent out scouting parties. These parties went as far west as the present-day states of California, Arizona, and New Mexico.

But, Coronado did not find the cities of gold. He did not even find great cities. All he found were villages of **Zuni** Indians.

Coronado and his men crossed the
Rio Grande River during their
exploration of the southwest.

These are the remains of the Kuaua pueblo. Coronado
stayed here during the winter of 1540.

The landscape of the southwest made travel hard for Coronado.

GRASS HUTS

Coronado decided to travel east. Again, his army crossed Texas. But, he still found no cities of gold.

Coronado headed north. He had heard of a city called **Quivira**. It was said that this city was filled with gold. Coronado found Quivira. But it was not a city of gold. It was only a small Indian village of grass huts.

Coronado found Indian villages but no gold.

RETURN TO NEW SPAIN

Coronado searched for two years. Finally, he returned to New Spain. The governor was not happy. He did not want to hear Coronado's stories of poor Indian villages. He wanted to see horses carrying bags of gold. But, Coronado never found the cities of gold. He had not found any gold at all.

Coronado explored much of the American southwest.

Coronado's Route
to Quivira

Quivira

New Spain
(Mexico)

NORTH AMERICA

The governor removed Coronado from his position of power. Coronado would no longer be the ruler of a territory. Instead, Coronado was given a job with very little power.

Coronado never found the Seven Cities of Gold.

NEVER AGAIN

Never again would Coronado lead an army of **explorers**. On September 22, 1554, Francisco Coronado died. He was 44 years old.

He never found riches for the **empire** of Spain. However, Coronado did explore much of North America. His travels took him thousands of miles across the New World.

Spain's interest in the New World led to Coronado's expedition.

IMPORTANT DATES TO REMEMBER

1510   Born in Spain

1540   Began search for the cities of gold

1542   Returned from unsuccessful expedition

1554   Died at age 44

GLOSSARY

empire (EM pyre) — a large kingdom or nation

expedition (EK spi dish un) — a journey

explorer (ek SPLOR er) — someone who travels to unknown places

Quivira (KEY vee rah) — a small Indian village

territory (TER eh tor ee) — an area of land

Zuni (ZOO nee) — a tribe of Native Americans

INDEX

Further Reading

Crisfield, Deborah. *The Travels of Francisco De Coronado.* Raintree
      Steck-Vaughn, 2001.

Jacobs, William J. *Coronado: A Dreamer in Golden Armor.* Econo-Clad Books, 1999.

Nardo, Don. *Francisco Coronado.* Franklin Watts, 2001.

Websites To Visit

http://www.encarta.com

http://www.pbs.org

About The Author

Trish Kline has written a great number of nonfiction books for the school and library market. Her publishing credits include two dozen books, as well as hundreds of newspaper and magazine articles, anthologies, short stories, poetry, and plays. She lives in Helena, Montana.